DATE:_____

Asshole of the Day

Today I'm Proud I Didn't...

Today I am Happy I Did...

I'm Lucky To Have

SUCCESSFUL PEOPLE DO WHAT THEY NEED TO DO
EVEN WHEN THEY DON'T FEEL LIKE IT. TOUGHEN UP.

Today's Shit List

PEOPLE, PLACES OR THINGS

- [ ] _____
- [ ] _____
- [ ] _____
- [ ] _____
- [ ] _____
- [ ] _____

Other Shit to Remember

DATE: _____

Asshole of the Day

Today I'm Proud I Didn't...

Today I am Happy I Did...

I'm Lucky To Have

DRAW SOME SHIT HERE

Today's Shit List
PEOPLE, PLACES OR THINGS

- ☐ _____
- ☐ _____
- ☐ _____
- ☐ _____
- ☐ _____
- ☐ _____
- ☐ _____
- ☐ _____
- ☐ _____
- ☐ _____

Other Shit to Remember

DATE: _____

Asshole of the Day

Today I'm Proud I Didn't...

Today I am Happy I Did...

I'm Lucky To Have

JUST PUNCH FEAR IN THE FUCKING FACE. THEN GO EAT A TACO.

Today's Shit List
PEOPLE, PLACES OR THINGS

- [ ] _____
- [ ] _____
- [ ] _____
- [ ] _____
- [ ] _____
- [ ] _____

Other Shit to Remember

Put Your Shit Down and Color

1. Slip a piece of paper behind the page your are coloring just to protect the pages behind from denting them if you have a heavy hand or bleed through issues.

2. Sharpen your pencil more than you think you need to.

this page intentionally left blank to prevent color bleeding.

DATE:_____

Asshole of the Day

Today I'm Proud I Didn't...

Today I am Happy I Did...

I'm Lucky To Have

Today's Shit List

PEOPLE, PLACES OR THINGS

- [ ] _____
- [ ] _____
- [ ] _____
- [ ] _____
- [ ] _____
- [ ] _____

Other Shit to Remember

Asshole of the Day

Today I'm Proud I Didn't...

Today I am Happy I Did...

I'm Lucky To Have

DRAW SOME SHIT HERE

Today's Shit List
PEOPLE, PLACES OR THINGS

- ☐ _____
- ☐ _____
- ☐ _____
- ☐ _____
- ☐ _____
- ☐ _____
- ☐ _____
- ☐ _____
- ☐ _____
- ☐ _____

Other Shit to Remember

Asshole of the Day

Today I'm Proud I Didn't...

Today I am Happy I Did...

I'm Lucky To Have

IF SOMEONE TELLS YOU "YOU CAN'T" THEY'RE
SHOWING YOU THEIR LIMITS. NOT YOURS!

Today's Shit List
PEOPLE, PLACES OR THINGS

- ☐ _____
- ☐ _____
- ☐ _____
- ☐ _____
- ☐ _____
- ☐ _____

Other Shit to Remember

this page intentionally left blank to prevent color bleeding.

DATE: _____

Asshole of the Day

_____

Today I'm Proud I Didn't...   ## Today I am Happy I Did...

_____

I'm Lucky To Have

_____

SHOULD. WOULD. COULD.
DID.

Today's Shit List

PEOPLE, PLACES OR THINGS

- [ ] _____
- [ ] _____
- [ ] _____
- [ ] _____
- [ ] _____
- [ ] _____

Other Shit to Remember

DATE:_____

Asshole of the Day

Today I'm Proud I Didn't...

Today I am Happy I Did...

I'm Lucky To Have

DRAW SOME SHIT HERE

Today's Shit List
PEOPLE, PLACES OR THINGS

- [ ] _____
- [ ] _____
- [ ] _____
- [ ] _____
- [ ] _____
- [ ] _____
- [ ] _____
- [ ] _____
- [ ] _____
- [ ] _____

Other Shit to Remember

DATE: _____

Asshole of the Day

Today I'm Proud I Didn't...

Today I am Happy I Did...

I'm Lucky To Have

DREAM + WORK = SUCCESS

Today's Shit List

PEOPLE, PLACES OR THINGS

- ☐ _____
- ☐ _____
- ☐ _____
- ☐ _____
- ☐ _____
- ☐ _____

Other Shit to Remember

DATE: _____

Asshole of the Day

Today I'm Proud I Didn't...

Today I am Happy I Did...

I'm Lucky To Have

REMEMBER WHEN YOU WANTED WHAT YOU CURRENTLY HAVE?

Today's Shit List

PEOPLE, PLACES OR THINGS

- ☐ _____
- ☐ _____
- ☐ _____
- ☐ _____
- ☐ _____
- ☐ _____

Other Shit to Remember

Asshole of the Day

Today I'm Proud I Didn't...

Today I am Happy I Did...

I'm Lucky To Have

DRAW SOME SHIT HERE

Today's Shit List
PEOPLE, PLACES OR THINGS

- [ ] _____
- [ ] _____
- [ ] _____
- [ ] _____
- [ ] _____
- [ ] _____
- [ ] _____
- [ ] _____
- [ ] _____
- [ ] _____

Other Shit to Remember

DATE:_____

Asshole of the Day

_____
_____
_____
_____
_____
_____
_____
_____

Today I'm Proud I Didn't...   ## Today I am Happy I Did...

I'm Lucky To Have

_____
_____
_____
_____
_____
_____

EVERYBODY CHANGES. NOW IT'S MY TURN

Today's Shit List

PEOPLE, PLACES OR THINGS

- [ ] _____
- [ ] _____
- [ ] _____
- [ ] _____
- [ ] _____
- [ ] _____

Other Shit to Remember

this page intentionally left blank to prevent color bleeding.

DATE: _____

Asshole of the Day

Today I'm Proud I Didn't...

Today I am Happy I Did...

I'm Lucky To Have

Today's Shit List
PEOPLE, PLACES OR THINGS

- ☐ _____
- ☐ _____
- ☐ _____
- ☐ _____
- ☐ _____
- ☐ _____

Other Shit to Remember

Asshole of the Day

Today I'm Proud I Didn't...

Today I am Happy I Did...

I'm Lucky To Have

DRAW SOME SHIT HERE

Today's Shit List
PEOPLE, PLACES OR THINGS

- ☐ _____
- ☐ _____
- ☐ _____
- ☐ _____
- ☐ _____
- ☐ _____
- ☐ _____
- ☐ _____
- ☐ _____
- ☐ _____

Other Shit to Remember

DATE: _____

Asshole of the Day

Today I'm Proud I Didn't...

Today I am Happy I Did...

I'm Lucky To Have

IF YOU ARE WAITING FOR A SIGN. THIS IS IT

Today's Shit List
PEOPLE, PLACES OR THINGS

- ☐ _____
- ☐ _____
- ☐ _____
- ☐ _____
- ☐ _____
- ☐ _____

Other Shit to Remember

this page intentionally left blank to prevent color bleeding.

DATE: _____

Asshole of the Day

Today I'm Proud I Didn't...

Today I am Happy I Did...

I'm Lucky To Have

RISK IS BETTER THAN REGRET..

Today's Shit List

PEOPLE, PLACES OR THINGS

- [ ] _____
- [ ] _____
- [ ] _____
- [ ] _____
- [ ] _____
- [ ] _____

Other Shit to Remember

Asshole of the Day

Today I'm Proud I Didn't...

Today I am Happy I Did...

I'm Lucky To Have

DRAW SOME SHIT HERE

Today's Shit List
PEOPLE, PLACES OR THINGS

☐ _____
☐ _____
☐ _____
☐ _____
☐ _____
☐ _____
☐ _____
☐ _____
☐ _____
☐ _____

Other Shit to Remember

Asshole of the Day

Today I'm Proud I Didn't...

Today I am Happy I Did...

I'm Lucky To Have

SUCCESS IS THE BEST REVENGE.

Today's Shit List
PEOPLE, PLACES OR THINGS

- [ ] _____
- [ ] _____
- [ ] _____
- [ ] _____
- [ ] _____
- [ ] _____

Other Shit to Remember

DATE:_____

Asshole of the Day

Today I'm Proud I Didn't...

Today I am Happy I Did...

I'm Lucky To Have

Today's Shit List

PEOPLE, PLACES OR THINGS

- [ ] _____
- [ ] _____
- [ ] _____
- [ ] _____
- [ ] _____
- [ ] _____

Other Shit to Remember

DATE: _____

Asshole of the Day

Today I'm Proud I Didn't...

Today I am Happy I Did...

I'm Lucky To Have

DRAW SOME SHIT HERE

Today's Shit List
PEOPLE, PLACES OR THINGS

- [ ] _____
- [ ] _____
- [ ] _____
- [ ] _____
- [ ] _____
- [ ] _____
- [ ] _____
- [ ] _____
- [ ] _____
- [ ] _____

Other Shit to Remember

DATE: _____

Asshole of the Day

Today I'm Proud I Didn't...

Today I am Happy I Did...

I'm Lucky To Have

BE THE WOMAN YOU NEEDED AS A GIRL.

Today's Shit List

PEOPLE, PLACES OR THINGS

- ☐ _____
- ☐ _____
- ☐ _____
- ☐ _____
- ☐ _____
- ☐ _____

Other Shit to Remember

this page intentionally left blank to prevent color bleeding.

DATE:_____

DAY OF THE WEEK
S M T W TH F S

Asshole of the Day

Today I'm Proud I Didn't...

Today I am Happy I Did...

I'm Lucky To Have

TRUST THE PROCESS

Today's Shit List
PEOPLE, PLACES OR THINGS

- [ ] _____
- [ ] _____
- [ ] _____
- [ ] _____
- [ ] _____
- [ ] _____

Other Shit to Remember

DATE: _____

Asshole of the Day

Today I'm Proud I Didn't...

Today I am Happy I Did...

I'm Lucky To Have

DRAW SOME SHIT HERE

Today's Shit List
PEOPLE, PLACES OR THINGS

- [ ] _____
- [ ] _____
- [ ] _____
- [ ] _____
- [ ] _____
- [ ] _____
- [ ] _____
- [ ] _____
- [ ] _____
- [ ] _____

Other Shit to Remember

DATE:_____

Asshole of the Day

Today I'm Proud I Didn't...

Today I am Happy I Did...

I'm Lucky To Have

YOUR BODY CAN STAND ALMOST ANYTHING. IT'S YOUR MIND THAT YOU HAVE TO CONVINCE.

Today's Shit List

PEOPLE, PLACES OR THINGS

- [ ] _____
- [ ] _____
- [ ] _____
- [ ] _____
- [ ] _____
- [ ] _____

Other Shit to Remember

this page intentionally left blank to prevent color bleeding.

DATE:_____

Asshole of the Day

Today I'm Proud I Didn't...

Today I am Happy I Did...

I'm Lucky To Have

STOP CHEATING ON YOUR FUTURE WITH YOUR PAST.
IT'S OVER.

Today's Shit List
PEOPLE, PLACES OR THINGS

- ☐ _____
- ☐ _____
- ☐ _____
- ☐ _____
- ☐ _____
- ☐ _____

Other Shit to Remember

DATE:_____

Asshole of the Day

Today I'm Proud I Didn't...

Today I am Happy I Did...

I'm Lucky To Have

DRAW SOME SHIT HERE

Today's Shit List
PEOPLE, PLACES OR THINGS

- ☐ _____
- ☐ _____
- ☐ _____
- ☐ _____
- ☐ _____
- ☐ _____
- ☐ _____
- ☐ _____
- ☐ _____
- ☐ _____

Other Shit to Remember

DATE:_____

Asshole of the Day

Today I'm Proud I Didn't...

Today I am Happy I Did...

I'm Lucky To Have

IMPRESS YOURSELF

Today's Shit List
PEOPLE, PLACES OR THINGS

- [ ] _____
- [ ] _____
- [ ] _____
- [ ] _____
- [ ] _____
- [ ] _____

Other Shit to Remember

this page intentionally left blank to prevent color bleeding.

Asshole of the Day

Today I'm Proud I Didn't...

Today I am Happy I Did...

I'm Lucky To Have

PRAY. WORK. SLAY.

Today's Shit List
PEOPLE, PLACES OR THINGS

- [ ]
- [ ]
- [ ]
- [ ]
- [ ]
- [ ]

Other Shit to Remember

DATE:_____

Asshole of the Day

Today I'm Proud I Didn't...

Today I am Happy I Did...

I'm Lucky To Have

DRAW SOME SHIT HERE

Today's Shit List
PEOPLE, PLACES OR THINGS

☐ _____
☐ _____
☐ _____
☐ _____
☐ _____
☐ _____
☐ _____
☐ _____
☐ _____
☐ _____

Other Shit to Remember

DATE: _____

Asshole of the Day

Today I'm Proud I Didn't...

Today I am Happy I Did...

I'm Lucky To Have

KINDNESS IS FREE. SPRINKLE THAT STUFF EVERYWHERE.

Today's Shit List
PEOPLE, PLACES OR THINGS

- ☐ _____
- ☐ _____
- ☐ _____
- ☐ _____
- ☐ _____
- ☐ _____

Other Shit to Remember

this page intentionally left blank to prevent color bleeding.

DATE: _____

Asshole of the Day

Today I'm Proud I Didn't...

Today I am Happy I Did...

I'm Lucky To Have

DARLING, YOU'RE A GODDESS, A BADASS AND YOU'RE TOTALLY GOT THIS.

Today's Shit List

PEOPLE, PLACES OR THINGS

- ☐ _____
- ☐ _____
- ☐ _____
- ☐ _____
- ☐ _____
- ☐ _____

Other Shit to Remember

Asshole of the Day

Today I'm Proud I Didn't...   Today I am Happy I Did...

I'm Lucky To Have

DRAW SOME SHIT HERE

Today's Shit List
PEOPLE, PLACES OR THINGS

- [ ] _____
- [ ] _____
- [ ] _____
- [ ] _____
- [ ] _____
- [ ] _____
- [ ] _____
- [ ] _____
- [ ] _____
- [ ] _____

Other Shit to Remember

Asshole of the Day

Today I'm Proud I Didn't...

Today I am Happy I Did...

I'm Lucky To Have

THE DISTANCE BETWEEN DREAM AND REALITY CALLED ACTION.

Today's Shit List

PEOPLE, PLACES OR THINGS

- [ ] _____
- [ ] _____
- [ ] _____
- [ ] _____
- [ ] _____
- [ ] _____

Other Shit to Remember

this page intentionally left blank to prevent color bleeding.

Asshole of the Day

Today I'm Proud I Didn't...

Today I am Happy I Did...

I'm Lucky To Have

THERE ARE 7 DAYS IN A WEEK, "SOMEDAY" ISN'T ONE OF THEM.

Today's Shit List

PEOPLE, PLACES OR THINGS

- ☐ _____
- ☐ _____
- ☐ _____
- ☐ _____
- ☐ _____
- ☐ _____

Other Shit to Remember

DATE:_____

Asshole of the Day

_____
_____
_____
_____
_____
_____
_____

Today I'm Proud I Didn't...   ## Today I am Happy I Did...

I'm Lucky To Have

_____
_____
_____
_____
_____

DRAW SOME SHIT HERE

Today's Shit List
PEOPLE, PLACES OR THINGS

- ☐ _____
- ☐ _____
- ☐ _____
- ☐ _____
- ☐ _____
- ☐ _____
- ☐ _____
- ☐ _____
- ☐ _____
- ☐ _____

Other Shit to Remember

DATE: _____

Asshole of the Day

Today I'm Proud I Didn't...

Today I am Happy I Did...

I'm Lucky To Have

ONCE IN A WHILE, BLOW YOUR OWN DAMN MIND.

Today's Shit List

PEOPLE, PLACES OR THINGS

- [ ] _____
- [ ] _____
- [ ] _____
- [ ] _____
- [ ] _____
- [ ] _____

Other Shit to Remember

Asshole of the Day

Today I'm Proud I Didn't...

Today I am Happy I Did...

I'm Lucky To Have

SEEK TO BE WHOLE, NOT PERFECT.

Today's Shit List
PEOPLE, PLACES OR THINGS

- ☐ _____
- ☐ _____
- ☐ _____
- ☐ _____
- ☐ _____
- ☐ _____

Other Shit to Remember

Asshole of the Day

Today I'm Proud I Didn't...

Today I am Happy I Did...

I'm Lucky To Have

DRAW SOME SHIT HERE

Today's Shit List
PEOPLE, PLACES OR THINGS

- ☐ _____
- ☐ _____
- ☐ _____
- ☐ _____
- ☐ _____
- ☐ _____
- ☐ _____
- ☐ _____
- ☐ _____
- ☐ _____

Other Shit to Remember

DATE:_____

Asshole of the Day

Today I'm Proud I Didn't...

Today I am Happy I Did...

I'm Lucky To Have

WAKE UP BEAUTY, IT'S TIME TO BEAST.

Today's Shit List

PEOPLE, PLACES OR THINGS

- ☐ _____
- ☐ _____
- ☐ _____
- ☐ _____
- ☐ _____
- ☐ _____

Other Shit to Remember

this page intentionally left blank to prevent color bleeding.

DATE: _____

Asshole of the Day

Today I'm Proud I Didn't...

Today I am Happy I Did...

I'm Lucky To Have

> IF YOU'RE TOO COMFORTABLE, IT'S TIME TO MOVE ON. TERRIFIED OF WHAT'S NEXT? YOU'RE ON THE RIGHT TRACK.

Today's Shit List

PEOPLE, PLACES OR THINGS

- ☐ _____
- ☐ _____
- ☐ _____
- ☐ _____
- ☐ _____
- ☐ _____

Other Shit to Remember

DATE:_____

Asshole of the Day

Today I'm Proud I Didn't...

Today I am Happy I Did...

I'm Lucky To Have

DRAW SOME SHIT HERE

Today's Shit List
PEOPLE, PLACES OR THINGS

- ☐ _____
- ☐ _____
- ☐ _____
- ☐ _____
- ☐ _____
- ☐ _____
- ☐ _____
- ☐ _____
- ☐ _____
- ☐ _____

Other Shit to Remember

DATE:_____

Asshole of the Day

Today I'm Proud I Didn't...

Today I am Happy I Did...

I'm Lucky To Have

Today's Shit List

PEOPLE, PLACES OR THINGS

- ☐ _____
- ☐ _____
- ☐ _____
- ☐ _____
- ☐ _____
- ☐ _____

Other Shit to Remember

this page intentionally left blank to prevent color bleeding.

Asshole of the Day

Today I'm Proud I Didn't...

Today I am Happy I Did...

I'm Lucky To Have

Today's Shit List

PEOPLE, PLACES OR THINGS

- ☐ _____
- ☐ _____
- ☐ _____
- ☐ _____
- ☐ _____
- ☐ _____

Other Shit to Remember

DATE: _____

Asshole of the Day

_____

Today I'm Proud I Didn't...

Today I am Happy I Did...

I'm Lucky To Have

DRAW SOME SHIT HERE

Today's Shit List
PEOPLE, PLACES OR THINGS

- ☐ _____
- ☐ _____
- ☐ _____
- ☐ _____
- ☐ _____
- ☐ _____
- ☐ _____
- ☐ _____
- ☐ _____
- ☐ _____

Other Shit to Remember

DATE:_____

Asshole of the Day

_____
_____
_____
_____
_____
_____
_____
_____

Today I'm Proud I Didn't...

Today I am Happy I Did...

I'm Lucky To Have

ANYTHING'S POSSIBLE IF YOU'VE GOT ENOUGH NERVE.

Today's Shit List

PEOPLE, PLACES OR THINGS

- ☐ _____
- ☐ _____
- ☐ _____
- ☐ _____
- ☐ _____
- ☐ _____

Other Shit to Remember

this page intentionally left blank to prevent color bleeding.

Asshole of the Day

Today I'm Proud I Didn't...

Today I am Happy I Did...

I'm Lucky To Have

YOU ARE BRAVER THAN YOU BELIEVE, STRONGER
THAN YOU SEEM AND SMARTER THAN YOU THINK.

Today's Shit List

PEOPLE, PLACES OR THINGS

- ☐ _____
- ☐ _____
- ☐ _____
- ☐ _____
- ☐ _____
- ☐ _____

Other Shit to Remember

DATE: _____

Asshole of the Day

_____

Today I'm Proud I Didn't...

Today I am Happy I Did...

I'm Lucky To Have

DRAW SOME SHIT HERE

Today's Shit List
PEOPLE, PLACES OR THINGS

☐ _____
☐ _____
☐ _____
☐ _____
☐ _____
☐ _____
☐ _____
☐ _____
☐ _____
☐ _____

Other Shit to Remember

DATE:_____

Asshole of the Day

Today I'm Proud I Didn't...

Today I am Happy I Did...

I'm Lucky To Have

STARVE YOUR DISTRACTIONS AND FEED YOUR FOCUS.

Today's Shit List

PEOPLE, PLACES OR THINGS

- ☐ _____
- ☐ _____
- ☐ _____
- ☐ _____
- ☐ _____
- ☐ _____

Other Shit to Remember

this page intentionally left blank to prevent color bleeding.

DATE:_____

Asshole of the Day

Today I'm Proud I Didn't...

Today I am Happy I Did...

I'm Lucky To Have

BE THE GAME CHANGER.

Today's Shit List
PEOPLE, PLACES OR THINGS

- ☐ _____
- ☐ _____
- ☐ _____
- ☐ _____
- ☐ _____
- ☐ _____

Other Shit to Remember

DATE:_____

Asshole of the Day

Today I'm Proud I Didn't...

Today I am Happy I Did...

I'm Lucky To Have

DRAW SOME SHIT HERE

Today's Shit List
PEOPLE, PLACES OR THINGS

☐ _____
☐ _____
☐ _____
☐ _____
☐ _____
☐ _____
☐ _____
☐ _____
☐ _____
☐ _____

Other Shit to Remember

DATE:_____

Asshole of the Day

Today I'm Proud I Didn't...

Today I am Happy I Did...

I'm Lucky To Have

I'M BUILDING A BRAND, I'M ALWAYS BUSY."

Today's Shit List

PEOPLE, PLACES OR THINGS

- ☐ _____
- ☐ _____
- ☐ _____
- ☐ _____
- ☐ _____
- ☐ _____

Other Shit to Remember

this page intentionally left blank to prevent color bleeding.

DATE:_____

Asshole of the Day

Today I'm Proud I Didn't...

Today I am Happy I Did...

I'm Lucky To Have

WHEN YOU LEARN HOW MUCH YOU'RE WORTH,
YOU'LL STOP GIVING PEOPLE DISCOUNTS.

Today's Shit List

PEOPLE, PLACES OR THINGS

- ☐ _____
- ☐ _____
- ☐ _____
- ☐ _____
- ☐ _____
- ☐ _____

Other Shit to Remember

DATE:_____

Asshole of the Day

Today I'm Proud I Didn't...

Today I am Happy I Did...

I'm Lucky To Have

DRAW SOME SHIT HERE

Today's Shit List
PEOPLE, PLACES OR THINGS

- ☐ _____
- ☐ _____
- ☐ _____
- ☐ _____
- ☐ _____
- ☐ _____
- ☐ _____
- ☐ _____
- ☐ _____
- ☐ _____

Other Shit to Remember

DATE:_____

Asshole of the Day

Today I'm Proud I Didn't...

Today I am Happy I Did...

I'm Lucky To Have

GOAL: TO MAKE AN INCOME WHILE MAKING AN IMPACT.

Today's Shit List

PEOPLE, PLACES OR THINGS

- [ ] _____
- [ ] _____
- [ ] _____
- [ ] _____
- [ ] _____
- [ ] _____

Other Shit to Remember

this page intentionally left blank to prevent color bleeding.

Asshole of the Day

Today I'm Proud I Didn't...

Today I am Happy I Did...

I'm Lucky To Have

BE SO GOOD THEY CAN'T IGNORE YOU.

Today's Shit List

PEOPLE, PLACES OR THINGS

- ☐ _____
- ☐ _____
- ☐ _____
- ☐ _____
- ☐ _____
- ☐ _____

Other Shit to Remember

DATE: _____

Asshole of the Day

Today I'm Proud I Didn't...

Today I am Happy I Did...

I'm Lucky To Have

DRAW SOME SHIT HERE

Today's Shit List
PEOPLE, PLACES OR THINGS

- [ ] _____
- [ ] _____
- [ ] _____
- [ ] _____
- [ ] _____
- [ ] _____
- [ ] _____
- [ ] _____
- [ ] _____
- [ ] _____

Other Shit to Remember

DATE:_____

Asshole of the Day

Today I'm Proud I Didn't...

Today I am Happy I Did...

I'm Lucky To Have

BLOSSOMING INTO A BADASS WOMAN WITH MORE FAITH THAN FEAR.

Today's Shit List

PEOPLE, PLACES OR THINGS

- [ ]
- [ ]
- [ ]
- [ ]
- [ ]
- [ ]

Other Shit to Remember

Made in the USA
Columbia, SC
04 August 2023

21212892R00085